1001 Wizard
Things to Spot

Gillian Doherty

Illustrated by Teri Gower

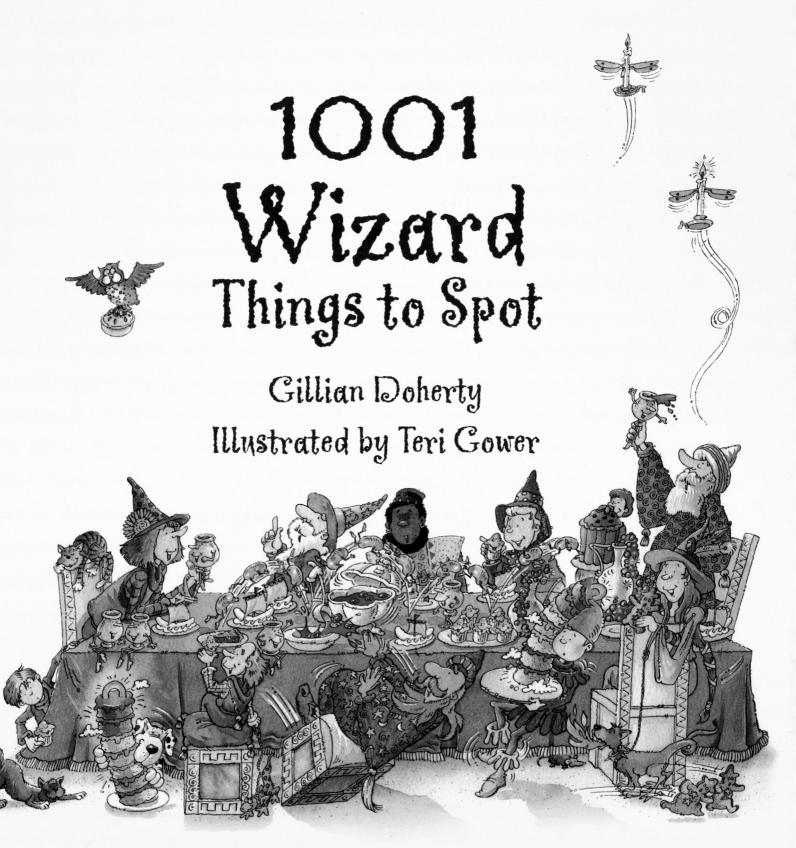

Designed by Teri Gower and Helen Wood
Edited by Anna Milbourne
Cover design by Russell Punter

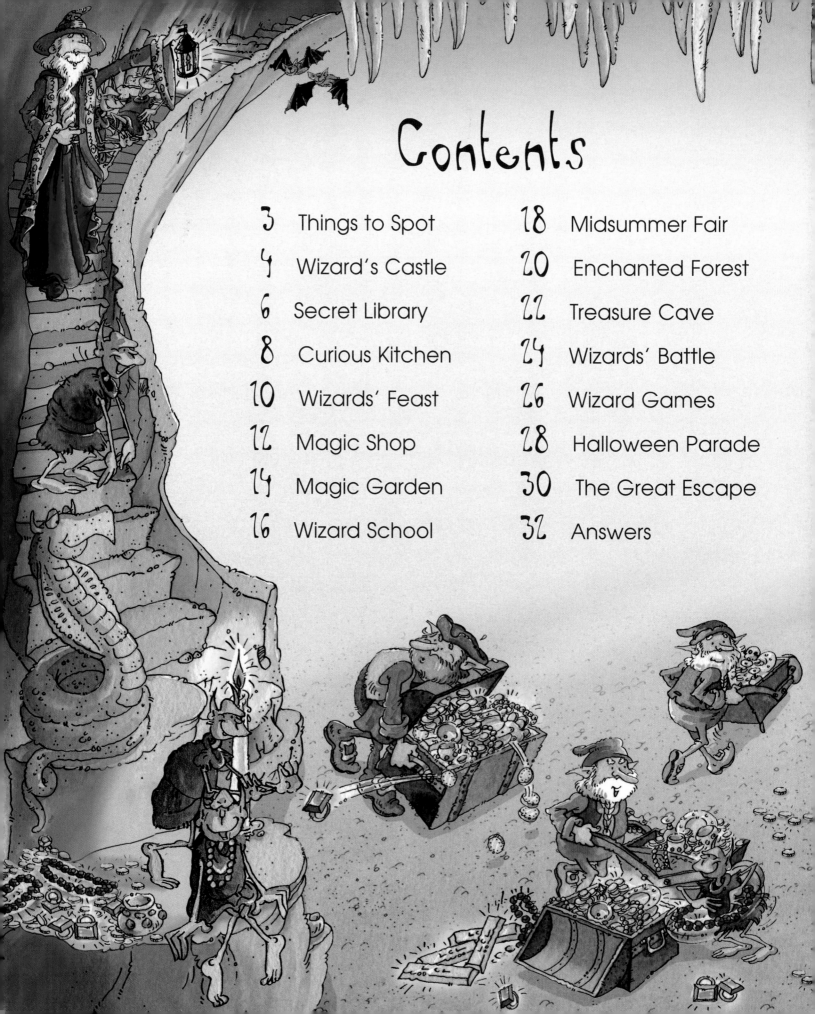

Contents

Things to Spot

Welcome to the magical world of wizards, where nothing is quite what it seems. In each scene there are all kinds of extraordinary things for you to find and count. There are 1001 things to spot altogether.

Wizard School

8 crooked wands

9 thinking caps

6 poison pens

9 tickling terrors

10 red spell books

4 shrunken elephants

1 wizard with donkey ears

10 spotted frogs

7 number crunchers

8 genies in bottles

Each little picture shows you what to look for in the big picture.

The number tells you how many of that thing you need to find.

16

17

Pip is a wizard's assistant. He's trying to learn all about magic, but it's not as easy as it looks. Can you find him in every scene?

Wizard's Castle

5 snappy crocodiles

6 dragons

7 hippogriffs

4 turrets with gold roofs

3 chimeras

9 troll guards

10 gargoyles

8 dream clouds

2 griffins

1 welcoming wizard

Secret Library

Astronom[y]

History

2 walkabout ladders

10 flying books

9 book pixies

4 wizards snoozing

1 grandfather clock

Meteorology

Botany

10 bookworms   7 ghosts   9 quill pens   8 spell scrolls   6 hedgehog paperweights

Curious Kitchen

10 runaway spoons
1 whistling kettle
5 cookbooks
7 busy brooms
9 soot imps

8 brownies

7 hungry mice

1 black cat

6 flame sprites

8 chocolate charm cakes

Wizards' Feast

9 spooky soufflés

10 flying candles

4 pumpkin pies

7 rainbow cakes

6 gingerbread wizards

8 magic muffins   9 talking goblets   10 jumping jellybeans   5 jugs of fizzy pop   7 banana boats

Magic Shop

7 sneaky spyglasses

8 flying boots

9 jars of dragons' teeth

6 warty toads

5 turbo broomsticks

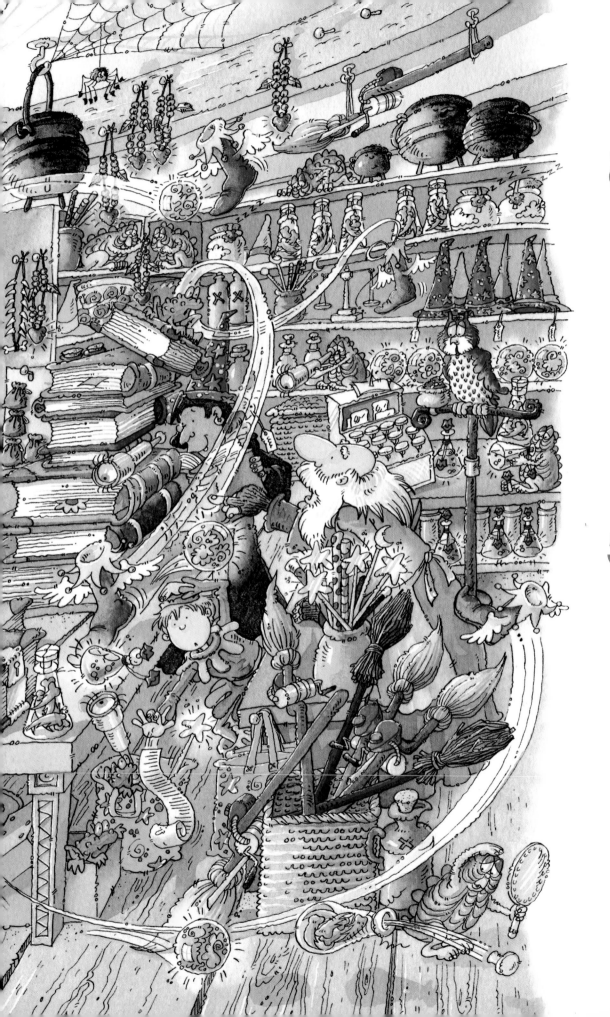

8 bottles of beauty potion

9 crystal balls

5 purple wizard hats

10 love charms

7 star wands

13

Magic Garden

7 fairies

9 mandrake plants

6 magic watering cans

8 snapdragons

9 venus flytraps

10 garden gnomes

7 money trees

1 wishing well

10 runner beans

2 firebirds

Wizard School

8 crooked wands

9 thinking caps

6 poison pens

9 tickling terrors

10 red spell books

16

4 shrunken elephants

1 wizard with donkey ears

10 spotted frogs

7 number crunchers

8 genies in bottles

Midsummer Fair

5 wizards in bumper cars

7 carousel horses

8 cuddly dragons

10 hoop snakes

9 hydra heads

1 bouncy castle

10 juggling balls

4 roperites

9 rubberadoes

10 swirly lollipops

Enchanted Forest

1 unicorn

8 forest elves

9 will-o'-the-wisps

7 grumpy dwarfs

4 trees with faces

 10 moon blooms
 9 toadstools
 8 star flowers
 10 tree sprites
 5 silver sickles

21

Treasure Cave

1 guard dragon

8 emerald rings

6 dwarfs with wheelbarrows

9 hobgoblins

10 gold bars

6 gold diggers

9 ruby necklaces

6 swords

8 treasure chests

7 stone serpents

Wizards' Battle

10 pixie pirates

8 shrieking squalls

7 sand boggles

9 brave starfish

5 seaweed monsters

1 spellbound
octopus

7 cowardly
crabs

8 sea
wizards

6 sea
dragons

9 shell
boats

Wizard Games

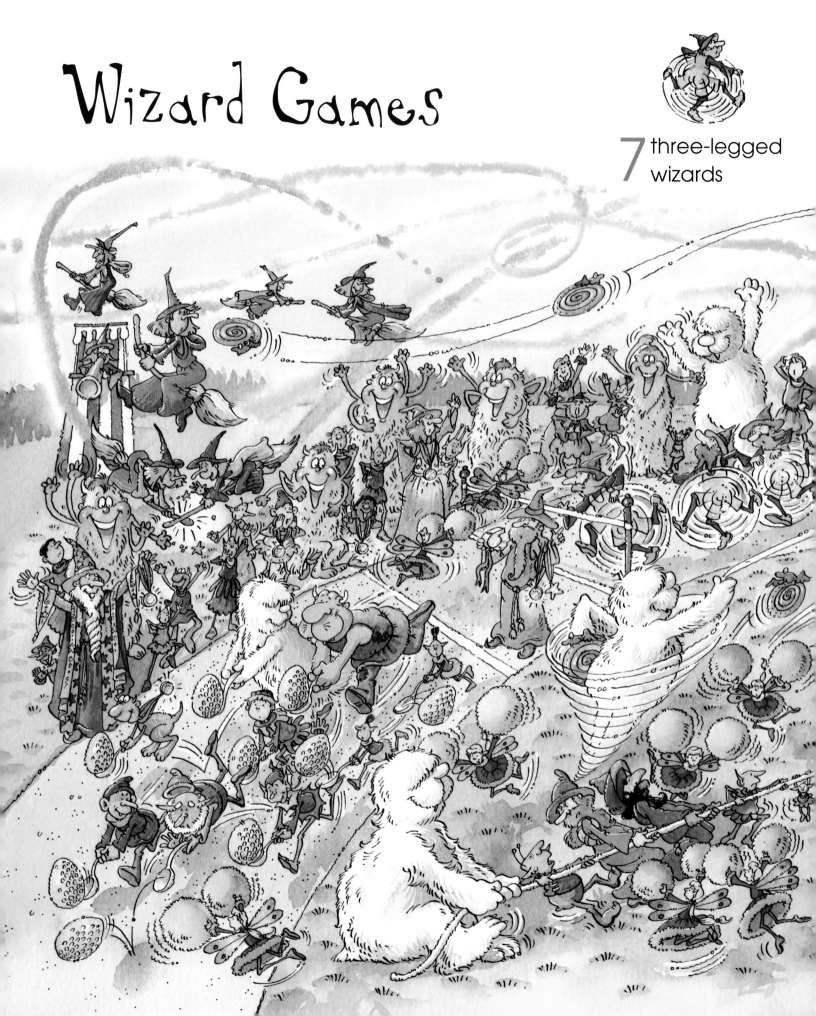

7 three-legged wizards

9 dragons' eggs

 6 whirling wibblers

 2 silver whistles

 8 gold medals

 10 magic arrows

 9 witches on broomsticks

 8 hullabaloos

 1 wizard on springs

 10 fairy cheerleaders

Halloween Parade

10 pumpkin lanterns

9 vampire bats

4 mummies

5 green ghouls

3 wizards in starry robes

9 naughty imps

7 skeletons

6 purple monsters

5 owls flying

6 spooky spirits

The Great Escape

Pip has forgotten to lock the stable doors and his master's magical beasts have escaped. Can you help him find them? They are hidden throughout the book.

10 water leapers

10 basilisks

7 centaurs

6 mugwumps

6 swagglers

8 squonks

9 gobblegonks

4 fauns

5 yetis

10 tripoderoos

6 werewolves

7 spriggans

9 burble boffins

31

Answers

Did you help Pip find all the magical beasts?
Here's where they are:

10 water leapers
Wizard's Castle
(pages 4–5)

10 basilisks
Magic Garden
(pages 14–15)

7 centaurs
Enchanted Forest
(pages 20–21)

6 mugwumps
Curious Kitchen
(pages 8–9)

6 swagglers
Wizards' Battle
(pages 24–25)

8 squonks
Magic Shop
(pages 12–13)

9 gobblegonks
Wizards' Feast
(pages 10–11)

4 fauns
Secret Library
(pages 6–7)

5 yetis
Wizard Games
(pages 26–27)

10 tripoderoos
Midsummer Fair
(pages 18–19)

6 werewolves
Halloween Parade
(pages 28–29)

7 spriggans
Treasure Cave
(pages 22–23)

9 burble boffins
Wizard School
(pages 16–17)

First published in 2007 by Usborne Publishing Ltd.,
Usborne House, 83-85 Saffron Hill, London EC1N 8RT, England. www.usborne.co.uk
Copyright © 2007, Usborne Publishing Ltd. The name Usborne and the devices ♀⊕ are Trade Marks of Usborne Publishing Ltd.
First published in America in 2008. UE. Printed in China.